I0137583

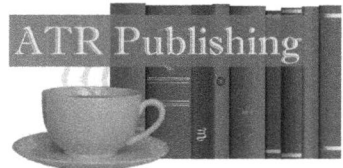

Wine, Food and Friends

by Chef Anne Marie

Published by:
ATR Publishing

Cover Photo by:
Ed Laymon

Back Cover Photo by:
Sherri Nicholas

ISBN: 978-0-9855835-3-8

Thank You

Thank you God for the gifts you have given me: family, friends, cooking, serving and all the gifts in my life.

Thank you to my husband, John, for encouraging me to do my best and be happy.

Thank you to my family for all your taste testing.

Thank you Dawn for editing and pushing me to go deeper.

Thank you Pat for all the hard work publishing and for hanging in there on me.

Table of Contents

Red and Green Appetizer Buffet

Paella Party

Sunday Dinner with the In-laws

Birthday Dinner

Dinner for Two by the Fire

Dinner on the Deck with Friends

Company in the Kitchen

Picnic at the Game

Salad Shower

Luncheon with the Ladies

Turkey for Thirty

Foreword

Think back to a fabulous time you had with your friends. Did you spend your time talking to them across a huge room? Probably not. Did you spend your time chatting while curled up in comfy chairs; perhaps across a dinner table or laughing on a barstool in a friend's kitchen? Some of my greatest memories with friends or family have been spent piled in a room or around a table, having fun conversations, laughing, eating and drinking yummy stuff. Entertaining doesn't have to be fancy. Coffee with muffins or wine and chips. It's about getting together.

I think you're getting the idea. When was the last time you had someone over? I really feel it is a lost art. Maybe it's because everyone tries to make it art. It should be relaxed and simple. What do you remember most? A dinner in a restaurant or a dinner someone took the time to make for you in a relaxed comfortable place?

My goal with this book is to spark an excitement in you to entertain. It's simpler than it sounds. Entertaining means a phone call, some cooking, some hellos and some laughs. The hardest part of that is the cooking. I have the cooking covered with this book! Read the menus, mix and match them, and get inspired. The recipes are simple enough for anyone to prepare, yet tasty enough for guests to enjoy.

One of my favorite things to do is have friends and family over. I love it. I hope you will, too. Thumb through Wine, Food, and Friends, and then give someone a call.

Now get cooking!

Before we start.....

A chef friend and I were talking and we both agreed that we wished all recipes were written like they were in college—it is much simpler and less intimidating. The more words the less likely people are willing to try the recipe. Yep, that's me! When I write recipes for myself, they usually look like code to the average cook.

Recipes should always have their ingredients listed in order of use. I always do this, so sometimes I don't need methods written out. If I am making cookies I know that the fat and sugar gets mixed first then add the eggs. Dry ingredients always mix together first before adding to wet and so on. I wrote the methods out for you, but kept it easy to read at a glance.

c = cup
T = Tablespoon
t = teaspoon
lb = pound

These are the way they were written in college and getting used to them will make your life simpler.

Read your whole recipe first to the end. I can't tell you how many times this has bit me. Just make yourself do it!

Mise en place. This French term is the key to hassle-free cooking. It translates to: "thing in its place". In the kitchen, it means to have things ready to go. I have written each recipe with this principle. If the ingredient list says "carrots, peeled and diced", then have them ready be-

fore you do anything else. If I am ready to get going on a method and I have to stop to peel and dice the carrots, it drives me crazy to have to stop what I'm doing to stop and peel and dice the carrots. I don't like cooking either under those conditions. It just feels like a whole lot of work. I simplified the methods to help you mise en place and you will love cooking much better.

Last, but not least, I had some fun with some of the recipes. I added some family humor for you. Feel free to laugh, I sure did.

Now get cooking and have some fun in the kitchen.

Red and Green Appetizer Buffet

Eye appeal is the theme! These recipes are a variation of some Christmas buffets that I have catered. In keeping with the red, green, and white scheme, you may switch in some of your favorite dishes. I find it best to combine simple- with hard-labor recipes to be realistic. It's your party and you should enjoy it if you want to!

All of these recipes can be made early in the day and most the day before. I usually put on a pot of hot spiced cider on to welcome my guests with a seasonal scent and to warm them from the inside out.

As for the wine, I recommend Davenport Cellars. Across the board, their wines are balanced, palate pleasers and are great for all year round. For this menu, they are perfect for three reasons: One, they have a white wine, named Snowflake, that is crisp and fitting; Two, they have mild and bold reds for your guest's varying tastes; and Three, all their wines, even their whites, are bottled in green glass to keep with your theme.

So, pour yourself a glass of your favorite beverage and be relaxed.

Red and Green Appetizer Buffet

🍷 Bacon Wraps

🍷 Cucumber Rolls

🍷 Pesto Pinwheels

🍷 Shrimp-Stuffed Tomatoes

🍷 Vegetables with Dill Dip

🍷 Meatballs with Debanne Sauce

🍷 Candy Cane Cupcakes

Bacon Wraps

Enough for 20 guests

---

2 packages Bacon, regular sliced not thick
2 cans Water Chestnuts, whole
1 ½ c Ketchup
½ c Sugar
½ c Brown Sugar
Box of Wooden Toothpicks

Preheat oven 350 degrees

---

1. Cut bacon in half to make twice as many pieces. Wrap piece around chestnut and toothpick to keep together. With toothpick standing up, place on baking sheet and bake 10 minutes. Remove wraps from oven and drain fat.

2. Mix ketchup and sugars in a small bowl. Using toothpicks as handles submerge wrap in ketchup, coating completely and place back on baking sheet.

3. Bake for 10 more minutes. Remove from oven and place on platter. Lightly cool for a couple of minutes, but serve while still hot.

Cucumber Roll

Enough for 20 guests

- 5 English Cucumbers, peeled
- 8 oz Cream Cheese
- 20 sprigs fresh Dill
- 2 T Johnny's Seasoning Salt
- Toothpicks

---

1. Slice cucumbers paper thin, lengthwise. A vegetable peeler works great or you may use a mandolin.

2. Lay cucumbers out flat on board and salt with Johnny's Seasoning Salt. Spread cream cheese on cucumber strips. If it is hard to mix, microwave for 25 seconds. Place a small dill sprig on end and roll strip up, keeping it tight with the sprig in the middle. If it hangs out a hair that is even better.

3. Toothpick and refrigerate for minimum of an hour before serving.

Can be made a day in advance—just be sure to cover.

Pesto Pinwheels

Enough for 20 guests

- 3 boxes or 6 sheets Puff Pastry, thawed
- 2 c Pesto
- 1 c Sundried Tomatoes, drained and chopped
- 2 Eggs, beaten

Preheat oven 400 degrees

---

1. Place the pastry sheet on floured surface and roll with a rolling pin to evenly make a larger piece.

2. From one end to ¾ of the way, spread ⅓ c pesto. Sprinkle 1/6 of tomatoes.

3. From the end of the dough that has the spread on it, roll tight, then stop where the dough does not have pesto and tomatoes on it. Brush the pastry that does not have any pesto on it with egg. Then finish rolling.

4. With the seam down, cut ½-inch slices and lay on greased, or papered and greased, baking sheet face up.

5. Bake for 25 to 30 minutes until golden and flaky. May be reheated for serving.

6. Serve warm on a platter.

Shrimp-Stuffed Tomatoes

Enough for 20 guests

- 40 Cherry Tomatoes, washed, stems removed
- 1 lb Salad Shrimp, rinsed
- 1 lb Sharp Cheddar Cheese, shredded
- 8 oz Parmesan Cheese, shredded
- 15 Black Olives, chopped
- ½ c Mayonnaise
- 1 t Salt
- ½ t Black Pepper
- ¼ c Parsley, fresh, chopped

---

1. With a small serrated knife, cut across very top of tomato and scoop out seeds.

2. In a small bowl, mix shrimp, cheeses, black olives, mayonnaise, salt and pepper.

3. With a spoon, fill tomatoes with shrimp mixture and place in baking dish.

4. Bake, to melt some cheese, but keep tomatoes intact. About 10 to 15 minutes.

5. Serve on platter. Top with fresh parsley.

Meat Balls with Debanne Sauce

Enough for 20 guests

- 3 lbs of Meatballs, cooked
- 2 T Olive Oil
- ¼ Onion, chopped
- 1 T Garlic, minced
- 1 c Ketchup
- 2 T Mustard
- ½ c Brown Sugar
- ¼ c Maple Syrup
- Salt and Pepper

Preheat oven 350 degrees

---

1. Place meatballs in a baking pan; bake covered until hot.
2. In a sauce pan, sauté onions in olive oil, over medium-low heat until onions are clear.
3. Add garlic, ketchup, mustard, brown sugar, syrup and simmer for 8 minutes.
4. Salt and pepper to taste.
5. Pour over meatballs and bake uncovered 10 minutes.

Sauce can be made ahead of time.

Candy Cane Cupcakes

Makes 24 cupcakes

- 1 box Chocolate Cake Mix
- 1 box Yellow Cake Mix
- ½ box Chocolate Pudding, instant
- 6 Eggs
- ¾ c Oil
- 2 ¼ c Water
- 2 T Red Food Coloring Gel
- 1 lb Butter, room temperature
- 2 lb Powdered Sugar
- 1 t Vanilla
- ½ t Almond Extract
- ½ t Salt
- 10 Candy Canes, crushed
- 24 Cupcake Papers, medium

Preheat oven 325 degrees

---

1. Mix water and food coloring.

2. In a mixer, combine cake mixes, eggs, oil, and water/ food coloring mixture at medium speed for 3 minutes.

3. Place cupcake papers in muffin tins. Fill cupcake papers, to ¾ full.

4. Bake 15 to 18 minutes until when touched, the cake will bounce like a sponge. Remove from oven.

5. While still hot, sprinkle with ½ candy canes to slightly melt to cake. Let cupcakes cool completely.

6. In a mixer, add butter, powder sugar, flavorings and salt. Mix slowly until smooth and creamy. I like to keep it pretty stiff if I use a knife to frost the cupcakes, but if I am piping with a bag I thin it a little with warm water.

7. Generously sprinkle remaining candy canes on top.

Paella Party

Tapas are popular right now, but the paella will be the star of the evening. In fact, the tapas page has been made easy and delicious to give you more time to focus on the whole menu and other recipes. Add in all sorts of colorful plates and transform your table to a setting in Spain.

The inspiration for this menu comes from several nights of Flying Dreams. No, I am not crazy! Flying Dreams is one of the tasty wineries in Woodinville, Washington, with whom I have been working. Leroy, the winemaker, introduced me to paella. His wines are Spanish style and a perfect accompaniment with this typical Spanish dish.

A lot of the paella recipes you can find are made with seafood. Flying Dreams serves this Chorizo and Smoked Chicken Paella at their wine release parties. Like Leroy, paella is so fun! Being taught how to make it on a grand scale for 30 to 100 people with a fancy pan, I decided to create a recipe to make at home. The selection of your pan is critical in order for it to cook evenly.

Having created other Spanish-themed dinners, all these recipes are tried and true. The Cookies with Wine are especially unique and yummy!

Paella Party

- Tapas (small plates)
- Orange Olive Salad
- Whole Herb-Stuffed Fish
- Chorizo and Smoked Chicken Paella
- Wine Ring Cookies

Tapas

Tapas means small plates and they are the perfect start to the evening.

Enough for 6 guests

- 6 oz Hummus
- 1 box Pita Crisps
- 1 can Almonds, blanched
- 1 jar stuffed Spanish Olives
- 6 oz Manchego Cheese, sliced
- 1 box Crackers

---

1. Place all ingredients on their own small plates. Relax and have fun.

Orange Olive Salad

Enough for 6 guests

- 3 Oranges, peeled, sliced
- 1 can Black Olives, small
- 1 small Red Onion, peeled, sliced thin
- 6 T Olive Oil
- 2 T Sherry Vinegar
- Salt and Pepper

---

1. On a platter arrange oranges.

2. Add olives, whole, randomly on top of the oranges.

3. Add onions randomly as well.

4. Sprinkle with oil and vinegar.

5. Salt and pepper to taste.

Whole Herb-Stuffed Fish

Enough for 6 guests

- 2 ½ lb Whole Fish, head on, cleaned, rinsed, your choice on type
- Salt and Pepper
- 4 Garlic Cloves, whole, peeled
- 1 Lemon, sliced
- 4 sprigs fresh Dill
- 4 sprigs fresh Thyme
- 4 sprigs fresh Sage
- 6 sprigs fresh Parsleys

---

1. Place whole fish on a foil-lined baking sheet. Salt and pepper inside of fish. Neatly layer remaining ingredients inside fish.

2. Place on the middle rack of oven. Broil on high, 7 to 8 minutes on each side.

3. Cut into 6 large slices, keeping center intact. Arrange on platter with more fresh herbs.

Chorizo and Smoked Chicken Paella

Enough for 6 guests

- 5 c Chicken Stock
- 2 Saffron Threads
- 1 small Onion, diced
- 3 T Olive Oil
- 2 lb Chicken Thighs, boneless, skinless, raw, smoked, chopped
- 1 lb Chorizo, Portuguese style, sliced
- 2 T Garlic, minced
- 2 c Bomba Rice
- 2 T Smoked Paprika
- 1 can Artichoke Hearts, quarters
- 1 small bag Peas, frozen
- 1 jar Red Peppers, roasted sliced

---

1. In a pot over medium heat, combined chicken stock and saffron threads.

2. In an extra-large skillet, add onion and oil. Sauté about 3 minutes over high heat. Add chicken and chorizo. Sauté about 5 minutes until chicken is almost cooked through. Add garlic and sauté 1 minute. Add rice, sauté 1 minute. Add saffron-chicken stock one cup at a time until rice is fully covered. Bring to a boil, give it

one final stir, and then add paprika over top.

3. Turn on to low and simmer 8 to 10 minutes. Do not stir! Good paella browns on the bottom. You may spoon more stock over top, if rice isn't cooking.

4. Place artichoke hearts across the top and simmer 5 minutes. Add peas on top and cook until rice is done and paella looks drier. Lay red peppers across the top and serve.

Wine Ring Cookies

Makes 4 dozen

- 1 ½ c Sugar, 1 c for baking, ½ c for tossing
- 1 c Vegetable Oil
- 1 c Butter, room temperature
- 1 T Baking powder
- 1 c White Wine
- 2 T Anise Extract
- 6 c Flour

Preheat oven to 325 degrees

---

1. With a mixer, combine 1 cup sugar, oil and butter. Add baking powder, wine and anise. After mixing well, add flour, 1 cup at a time, mixing well between cups.

2. When all is incorporated, measure out ¼ cup. On a non-floured cutting board roll in to a 12 inch rope. Cut into thirds. Bend so that its tips meet, creating a doughnut shape. Place on an ungreased cookie sheet.

3. Repeat for rest of dough, measuring out ¼ cup at a time. 12 should fit on a standard pan.

4. Bake for 15 to 17 minutes, until bottom is slightly colored.

5. Let cool on cookie sheet for 3 to 4 minutes.

6. Toss gently with ½ cup sugar.

7. Add salt and pepper to taste

Enjoy.

Note: Can be made up to 24 hours in advance.

Sunday Dinner with the In-laws

On Sundays, I enjoy big dinners with little work! This menu is one of my favorites. With a little planning ahead, you will feel at ease with the in-laws.

I really enjoy my in-laws. Being able to pre-make as much as I can on Friday or Saturday and just putting it in the slow cooker on Sunday opens the whole day for visiting. As a bonus, there are usually leftovers for one of the weeknights, as well.

While the guys watch the game downstairs, we have a chick flick on upstairs. I say "on" because we are usually too busy visiting to watch the whole movie. When the men finally emerge, dinner is ready in a snap. With a pop of the cork, a whole new party begins around the table.

For this menu, I have Alta Cellars on hand. Alta does a super job with their Bordeaux-inspired wines. It is an excellent fit for a slow cooked meal and a laidback day.

Oh, and if you're not as lucky as I am to have awesome in-laws, friends will work!

Who wouldn't want to start your week this way?

Sunday Dinner with the In-Laws

Hot Artichoke Dip

Salad with Vinaigrette and Handmade Croutons

Slow Cooker Beef Stroganoff

Pumpkin Pie Cake

Hot Artichoke Dip

Enough for 4 guests

- 1 c Artichoke Hearts, quartered
- 1 c Mayonnaise
- ½ c Onion, chopped
- ¼ c Parsley, fresh, chopped
- ½ c Parmesan Cheese, shredded (two ¼ c portions)
- 1 loaf French Bread, sliced

Preheat oven to 350 degrees

---

1. In a baking dish combine artichokes, mayonnaise, onion, parsley and ¼ c cheese.

2. Sprinkle ¼ c cheese over top and bake for 30 minutes.

3. Serve warm with French bread.

Salad with Vinaigrette and Handmade Croutons

Enough for 4 guests

- 3 slices Bread, cubed
- 1 T Olive Oil
- 1 T Butter, melted
- ½ t Garlic Salt
- ½ t Italian Seasoning
- 1 T Shallot, finely minced
- 1 t Dijon Mustard
- 2 t Red Wine Vinegar
- ¼ c Olive Oil
- 1 t Sugar
- 1 t Honey
- Salt and Ground Black Pepper
- 4 c Salad Greens

Preheat oven to 350

1. In a medium bowl, mix oil and butter. Toss in bread cubes.

2. On a baking sheet, place bread cubes and sprinkle with garlic salt and Italian seasoning.

3. Bake about 8 to 10 minutes until dry and toasted.

4. Remove from oven and leave on baking sheet until cooled.

5. Combine the shallot, mustard, vinegar, oil, sugar, honey and salt and pepper in a jar and shake to emulsify.

6. Toss with salad greens.

7. Top with cooled croutons.

Slow Cooker Beef Stroganoff

Enough for 4 guests

- 2 lb Flank or Round Steak, sliced to ¼-inch thick strips
- 2 c Beef Stock
- ½ c Onion, chopped
- 1 T Garlic, minced
- 1 ½ lb Mushrooms, sliced
- ½ c Sour Cream
- 6 c Egg Noodles, cooked and drained
- Salt and Pepper

---

1. In a sauce pan, brown steak and then place in slow cooker.

2. Pour stock into pan to deglaze and then add to slow cooker.

3. Add onion and garlic to slow cooker and turn on to low.

4. Cook for 6 to 8 hours.

5. Add mushrooms and cook 1 more hour.

6. Add sour cream, noodles, salt and pepper, then serve hot.

Pumpkin Pie Cake

Enough for 4 guests

- 15 oz can Pumpkin
- 2 Eggs
- ¾ c Sugar
- 2 T Cinnamon
- 2 t Nutmeg
- 2 t Ginger
- ½ t Clove
- 8 oz Canned Milk
- ½ box Yellow Cake Mix
- ½ cube Butter, melted
- ½ c Coconut
- ½ c Walnuts, chopped

Preheat oven to 350 degrees

---

1. In a medium bowl, add pumpkin, eggs, sugar, cinnamon, nutmeg, ginger, cloves and canned milk. Mix with mixer well.

2. Pour into 9 x 13 cake pan.

3. Sprinkle dry cake mix over pumpkin mixture.

4. Drizzle butter over top of cake mix. Sprinkle on coconut, then walnuts.

5. Bake for 30 to 40 minutes.

Serve warm or cold.

Birthday Dinner

Growing up, my mom always let us pick our birthday dinner. It was the most exciting thing, if we wanted salad and cold cereal, the whole family sat down to just that!

My favorite was spaghetti, salad, and pumpkin pie. Now, more than twenty years after my mom has passed, I still find comfort in that birthday dinner.

The menu on the next page is my youngest child's usual choice. I chose these recipes because they are good, basic recipes and they always make me think of my 6-foot 2-inch little buddy. The salad is his favorite and his great-aunt from Germany taught me the apple bacon toast. The schnitzel is something his dad's mother taught me and the whip cream frosting is something my mom always made.

This one's for you, Skyler. Thanks for being my best critic!

Birthday wine must be great! When customers ask what a good wine to give is, I say the wines at Kaella Winery are always a big hit. They are award winning as well as good drinkers. Kaella is one of the ones at the top of my list.

Birthday Dinner

🍷 Bacon Apple Toast

🍷 Green Salad with Thousand
Island Dressing

🍷 Crispy Smashed Potatoes

🍷 Schnitzel

🍷 Chocolate Cake and
Whipped Cream Frosting

Bacon Apple Toast

Enough for 8 guests

- ½ French Bread Baguette, 2 or 3 inches in diameter, sliced ¼-in. thick (12 slices)
- 6 Bacon Slices, apple smoked, cut in half
- 1 T Lemon Juice
- 1 Apple, peeled, cored, sliced and rubbed with lemon juice
- 3 oz Sharp Cheddar Cheese, shredded

---

1. Preheat oven 350 degrees

2. Place French bread slices on a baking sheet and lightly toast both sides.

3. Place apple and then bacon on toast. Be sure to cover bread completely or the edges will burn.

4. Bake 10 minutes.

5. Remove from oven to turn bacon over.

6. At this point, you can put these in the refrigerator and finish the last 10 minutes before your party.

7. Bake another 8 minutes.

8. Cover with cheese.

9. Bake until melted about, 2 minutes.

Homemade Thousand Island Dressing

Makes 1 ½ cups

- 1c Mayonnaise
- 3 T Ketchup
- 3 T Sweet Relish
- ½ t Mustard
- 1 ½ t Black Pepper, ground
- 1 t Salt
- 1 t Lemon juice
- ¼ t Paprika

---

1. In a small bowl combine all ingredients and mix well.

If you like a thinner dressing, add milk.

Crispy Smashed Potatoes

Makes enough for 8 guests

- 16 Yukon Gold Potatoes, washed
- ¼ c Olive Oil
- 2 t Sea Salt

Preheat oven 350 degrees

---

1. Place potatoes on a baking sheet and bake until soft to touch, about 45 min to 1 hour.

2. Remove from oven and with a paper towel, folded in fourths, on the palm of your hand, press it flat.

3. Drizzle with olive oil

4. Bake another 10 to 15 minutes until slightly crispy.

5. Season with salt

Enjoy hot!

Schnitzel

Enough for 8 guests

- 3 lb Pork Loin, sliced into 8 pieces
- 1 c Flour
- 3 Eggs, beaten
- 3 T Water
- 3 c Seasoned Bread Crumbs
- 4 c Vegetable Oil
- 2 Lemons, wedged

Preheat oven 300 degrees

---

1. To get started, layout three shallow dishes as a breading station. Fill the first dish with flour, the second with eggs and water mixed together, and the third with bread crumbs. Place a baking sheet in the oven.

2. On a cutting board, butterfly each piece of pork loin. (Slice each piece of meat as if you were going to slice it again, but stop ⅞ of the way down.) Open it like a butterfly on the board.

3. Pound each butterflied pork loin with a meat hammer on both sides.

4. Bread the pork at the breading station on both sides. First in the flour, then in the egg mixture, and lastly in

the breadcrumbs.

5. Preheat oil in a large heavy pan on medium high.

6. Fry breaded pork, a couple at a time, in oil, until golden brown.

7. Blot on paper towel and place in oven on the baking sheet.

Serve with a lemon wedge to squeeze over the meat.

Wash your hands after every major task and wash all surfaces well. You must be careful with raw pork.

Chocolate Cake with Whipped Cream Frosting

Makes enough for 10 guests

- 2 c Sugar
- 1 ¾ c Flour
- ¾ c Cocoa Powder
- 2 t Baking Soda
- 1 t Baking Powder
- 1 t Salt
- 2 Eggs
- 1 c Buttermilk
- 1 c Coffee, strong
- ½ c Vegetable Oil
- 2 t Vanilla
- 4 c Whipping Cream, whipped
- 1 box Chocolate Pudding, instant

Preheat oven 350 degrees

---

1. Place parchment paper in bottom of baking pan. It's your preference on the pans you need depending on your occasion.

2. In a large bowl, mix sugar, flour, cocoa, soda, baking powder and salt. Add eggs, buttermilk, coffee, oil and

vanilla. Beat with mixer on medium speed for 2 to 3 minutes until smooth. Batter will be thin.

3. Pour into pan or pans evenly.

4. Bake 30 to 40 minutes until you can push a toothpick in the center of the cake and it comes out clean.

5. Let cake rest on cooling rack 5 minutes then run knife around outside to release. Invert onto your platter and let cool completely.

6. In a large bowl, mix whipped whipping cream and pudding, right out of the box, with a mixer until smooth.

A hot cake, tightly wrapped with plastic wrap or foil, which is placed in the freezer will not only cool quicker, but will retain its moisture and taste better, too.

Only frost a cooled cake.

Dinner for Two by the Fire

Imagine an evening with the television off and a fire burning. You're chatting and relaxing on a rainy evening.

Ok, so I am a hopeless romantic.

This menu can be eaten anywhere, but I recommend this way: Be prepared hours before, pop the rolls in before your guest arrives, use the bake time to get ready, and you will enjoy your evening like a guest.

It's all about the chatting and the warming from the inside out.

Storm Front Wine… You won't only love the names to accompany this evening but the wines are also amazing. Convergence Zone Cellars are award-winning wines that would fit this evening like the warmth of a fire on a cold night. It may just become one of your favorites too.

Dinner for Two by the Fire

🍷 Shrimp Stack with Cocktail Sauce

🍷 Beet Salad

🍷 Butternut Squash Soup

🍷 Herb Buttered Rolls

🍷 Caramel Corn

Shrimp Stack with Cocktail Sauce

Enough for 8 guests

- 8 oz Cream Cheese
- 1 lb Salad Shrimp, rinsed and towel-dried
- 1c Cocktail Sauce (see recipe below)
- 6 oz Sharp Cheddar Cheese, shredded
- 3 Green Onions, cleaned and chopped
- 1 box of your favorite Crackers

---

1. On a medium platter, spread cream cheese. Pile the shrimp in the center. Pour the cocktail sauce over the shrimp. Spread the cheese over the sauce. Sprinkle the Green Onions on top.

2. Serve with Crackers.

Cocktail Sauce

- ¾ c Ketchup
- 2 T Horseradish
- 2 T Lemon Juice

---

1. In a small bowl, add all ingredients and mix well.

Beet Salad

Enough for 2 people

Can be made up to 24 hours in advance

- 4 Roasted Red Beets, sliced
- 1 Naval Orange, peeled and sliced
- 1 T Olive Oil
- ¼ c Walnuts, rough chopped
- ¼ c Gorgonzola Crumbles
- Salt & Pepper

---

1. Place all ingredients in bowl. Toss lightly. Add salt and pepper to taste.

Butternut Squash Soup

Makes 5 cups of soup

- 3 c roasted Butternut Squash
- 2 T Olive Oil
- ½ small Onion, diced small
- 2 c Chicken Stock
- 1 ½ t Curry Powder
- Salt and Pepper

---

1. In a stock pot, cook olive oil and onions over medium-high heat. Sauté until clear.

2. Add roasted squash and chicken stock to pot. Bring to a simmer, just before a boil.

3. Use an immersion blender or place in a blender to puree. Caution! It is hot and you need a towel to hold down the cap of the blender or the puree will fly up and burn you. Note: For a cream soup option, 3 T heavy cream may be stirred in after soup is pureed.

4. Add curry, salt and pepper to taste.

This delicious soup may be prepared far ahead of time, then reheated.

Herb-Buttered Rolls

- Dinner roll dough, from the freezer section, follow thawing and raising directions
- ½ lb Butter, salted, room temperature
- 1 t Garlic Powder
- 1 t Oregano, fresh, chopped
- ½ t Rosemary, fresh, chopped

1. Place all in ingredients in bowl. Mix with mixer or strong spoon.

2. Place on parchment paper or wax paper in a log shape. Roll and seal.

3. Refrigerate for at least 1 hour.

4. Slice into desired serving size. (At this point, Herb-Buttered Rolls may be stored in freezer up to 6 months in advance.)

5. Bake Rolls according to package directions.

Enjoy your warm, fresh rolls with this high-flavored butter. Your home will smell great, too!

Caramel Corn

- 2 bags of microwave Popcorn
- 1 c Brown Sugar
- ¼ c Corn Syrup
- ½ c Butter
- ½ t Salt
- 1 tsp Vanilla
- ½ tsp Baking Soda

1. Pop 2 bags of microwave Popcorn. Set aside in a large paper bag Note: May be kept warm in a 200 degree oven.

2. In a large glass bowl, combine brown sugar, corn syrup, butter, and salt. Microwave for 90 seconds, stir, then microwave for another 90 seconds, then stir again.

3. Add vanilla and baking soda. It will foam. After mixed well, pour over popcorn in bag. Shake well. Microwave 1 minute, shake bag. Repeat

4. Microwave again for 30 sec. / shake / repeat

5. Pour onto cookie sheet and enjoy when cool enough!

Dinner on the Deck with Friends

Entertaining on the deck or patio is so much fun. The relaxed atmosphere allows you to do a lot of the cooking while enjoying your guests. Pre-making as much as you can and setting yourself up with a mini kitchen (table) next to the grill will add more fun for you at the party.

And don't forget the drinks! A drink station with options will keep your guests refreshed as well as keeping you on task with time to talk.

If you can talk a partner or friend to grill with you the party will gather. Hanging out with good friends and good food is the great for making memories.

Every summer we have a grilling event at Cuillin Hills Winery. Derek is fun and his wines pair perfectly with most grilled foods. I highly recommend Cuillin Hills wine for this menu.

Friends on the Deck

- Chilled Bing Cherry Soup
- Garden Greens with Blender French Dressing
- Grilled Eggplant
- Grilled Smashed Baby Potatoes
- Fresh Herb Macerated Rib Roast
- Caramelized Pear Cake

Chilled Bing Cherry Soup

Makes 8 cups

- 2 c Water
- 1 c Muscat (sweet white wine)
- 3 T Lemon Juice
- 1 t Lemon Zest
- ¾ c Sugar
- 4 Peppercorns
- 6 Cloves, whole
- 1 Cinnamon stick
- 6 c Bing Cherries, pitted
- 1 T Cornstarch
- 6 T Sour Cream

---

1. In a stock pot, combine water, wine, lemon juice, lemon zest, sugar, and spices. Bring to a boil, then add pitted cherries. Bring back to a boil.

2. Remove from heat and cover. Allow to steep, off the heat, 30 minutes.

3. Remove the spices from the cherries and reserve 18 cherries for garnish.

4. Strain the juice and reserve.

5. Puree Cherry's and add back to juice.

6. Bring back to boil

7. Dissolve cornstarch 1 tablespoon cold water. Boil 2 minutes

8. Serve chilled and garnish with reserved cherries and sour cream.

Blender French Dressing

Makes 3 cups

- 1 c Olive Oil
- 1 c Ketchup
- ½ c Sugar
- ¼ c White Vinegar
- ¼ c Water
- 1 t Garlic Salt
- 1 t Black Pepper
- ¼ t Salt

---

1. Blend all ingredients in a blender for 2 minutes.

Grilled Eggplant

Enough for 8 guests

- 2 Eggplants, large
- ½ c Olive Oil
- 1 t Salt
- ½ c Parmesan Cheese, shredded

---

1. Slice eggplant to ½ inch thick. Salt on both sides. Place on baking sheet. Sprinkle ½ of olive oil over slices.

2. On a hot grill or grill pan, sear slices to heat through. Remove when eggplant starts to look wet. Lay flat back on baking sheet and sprinkle with olive oil and cheese.

3. Serve warm on a platter.

Grilled Smashed Baby Potatoes

Enough for 8 guests

- 3 to 4 lb Baby Potatoes, washed, tri color is nice
- 1 c Sour Cream
- 2 T Chives, fresh, Chopped
- 1 T Garlic, minced
- Salt and Pepper

Preheat oven 400 degrees

---

1. Place potatoes on baking sheet and bake until soft to touch, 40 to 60 minutes depending on size of potato. Cool in refrigerator at least 2 hours or more hours, can be overnight.

2. In a small bowl, mix sour cream, chives and garlic.

3. On a hot grill, place cooled potatoes. Rotate while heating through center. Remove from grill and press flat with metal spatula.

4. Top with a dollop of sour cream mixture and salt and pepper.

Enjoy while warm.

Fresh Herb Macerated Rib Roast

Enough for 8 guests

- 3 lb Rib Roast
- 3 T Tri Pepper Seasoning
- 2 T Sea Salt
- ¼ lb Butter, melted
- 3 T Garlic, minced
- 1 bunch Rosemary
- 1 bunch Parsley
- 1 bunch Thyme
- ½ bunch Sage

Preheat oven to 400 degrees

---

1. Coat roast with tri pepper and sea salt. In a roasting pan, on a rack with a small amount of water in bottom of pan, bake roast uncovered for 25 to 30 minutes until roast has internal temperature of 130 degrees.

2. Preheat grill, you will need it to be hot!

3. Add garlic and butter into a small pan.

4. Gather ½ of each herb into a bouquet. Tie string tight around base to create an herb brush. Place pan of garlic butter to back or side of grill. Place herb brush top down into butter to rest.

5. Remove stems from remaining herbs and place on cutting board.

6. Remove roast from oven and immediately place on hot grill. Using herb brush, rub roast with butter a couple times while roast comes to an internal temperature of 140.

7. Remove roast from grill and lay on cutting board over herbs. Drizzle with olive oil. Place some herbs on top of roast and let rest 5 minutes.

8. Slice roast with macerated herbs still connected.

Caramelized Pear Cake

- 1 c Flour
- ¼ c Brown Sugar
- 1 t Baking Powder
- 1 t Cinnamon, ground
- 1 t Ginger, ground
- ¼ t Baking Soda
- ¼ t Salt
- ¼ t Cloves, ground
- ½ c Buttermilk
- 1 Egg, Large
- ½ stick (¼ c) Butter, melted
- ¼ c Molasses
- 1 T Butter
- ⅓ c Brown Sugar
- ¼ c Walnuts, chopped
- 2 Pears, cored, peeled and thinly slices

Preheat oven 375 degrees

1. In a large bowl, mix buttermilk, eggs, butter and molasses.

2. In a smaller bowl, mix flour, brown sugar, baking powder, cinnamon, ginger, baking soda, salt and ground cloves.

3. Add flour mixture to buttermilk mixture and stir until smooth.

4. In a heavy skillet, melt butter and brown sugar. Cook bubbling mixture for one minute, then remove from heat. Add walnuts. Arrange pear slices in the pan on top of nuts. Pour batter over pears.

5. Bake 30 minutes or until toothpick goes in center and comes out clean.

6. Cool on rack 10 minutes. Place platter over pan and invert.

7. Serve warm with ice cream.

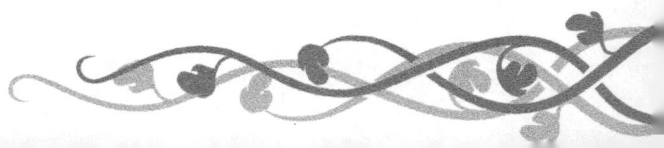

Company in the Kitchen

I love having parties, but it was hard in the beginning. I had a picture in my mind of how things would look and work, but nothing ever went as planned. I could set food in the dining room but still everyone hung in the kitchen with the mess. So I decided to embrace it. I created a Kitchen Party. It was a great way to have nibbles, drinks and fun with your friends. It also helped me get comfortable with people in my kitchen. These are now some of my favorite parties.

To get prepared for the party is simple. Long before the party, do the messy stuff: make the dips, set out the dishes, and anything else with which you feel you will struggle. Refresh yourself one hour before the party, then and relax. When it's time for your guests to arrive, be in the kitchen cooking or chopping. They will join you and the party will unfold. Set out new things to eat at random throughout the night and your guests will be amazed.

Don't forget to set the scene with candles, music and some jazzy wine.

Darren Des Voigne is the winemaker at Des Voigne Cellars. He makes a good variety of wines, which not only have amazingly full flavor, but the jazzy labels add to your party's atmosphere.

I hope you will invite company into your kitchen!

Company in the Kitchen

Sausage Board

Salmon Pate

Bruschetta

Small Plates

Fruit and Mello Dip

Sausage Board

Makes enough for 8 guests

- 1 Kielbasa, smoked and fully cooked
- 1 French Bread Dough, your recipe or Pillsbury
- Mustard, a couple different of your favorite types, in small cups
- Cheese, Olives, Pickled Vegetables or whatever you would like to put with it.

Preheat oven 350 degrees

---

1. Boil a large pot of water. Cut a slit down the length of the Kielbasa. Boil in water for 3 to 4 minutes. Remove from the water and remove casing from Kielbasa. Cool Kielbasa.
2. On a floured surface, press dough with the palm of your hand, into a large rectangle. Lay Kielbasa on top and wrap with dough. Place on a baking sheet with seam on bottom.
3. Bake 20 to 30 minutes until bread is golden brown.
4. Slice into thick chunks. Place on board or large oval platter with other items.
5. I like to place the pieces of breaded kielbasa back in the original shape?

Salmon Pâté

Makes 16 ounces

- 8 oz Cream Cheese
- 8 oz Smoked Salmon, boneless
- 2 T Lemon Juice
- 1 T Garlic, minced
- 1 T Hickory Smoked Flavoring

---

1. In a food Processor or strong mixer, mix all ingredients until smooth.

2. Serve with crackers

I like to form the pate into a shape on plate and garnish with dill.

Bruschetta

Makes about 3 ½ cups

- 6 large Tomatoes, diced
- 6 large Basil leaves, thinly sliced
- 4 T Olive Oil
- 2 T Balsamic Vinegar
- Salt and Pepper
- Loaf of French Bread, sliced and toasted

---

1. In a large bowl mix ingredients. Season with salt and pepper. Serve at room temperature on bread.

Store in refrigerator.

Small Plates

I like to set small plates of finger foods that are tasty and easy to assemble, amongst the other food.

Some ideas...

- Cream cheese with pepper jelly
- Nuts
- Figs with honey and walnuts
- Marinated artichokes
- Dried fruits
- Chocolates

What's in your panty?

Fruit and Mello Dip

Makes enough for 8 guests

- 6 oz Cream Cheese
- 6 oz Marshmallow Cream
- 2 Apples, cored, sliced and tossed with lemon juice
- 1 jar Maraschino Cherries
- 1 lb Grapes, rinsed and made into small clusters

---

1. In a medium bowl, microwave cream cheese 45 seconds to soften.

2. Remove Marshmallow lid and microwave jar for 30 seconds to soften.

3. Mix the two together and refrigerate 20 minutes.

4. Arrange apples, cherries and grapes on platter and serve with chilled dip.

Picnic at the Game

Homecoming can be so fun! A girlfriend and I used to meet at the game with a picnic for ourselves. I really looked forward to it every year. A combination of handy snacks, comfort food, and a warm drink hits the spot on a chilly night in the bleachers.

Hot cocoa with your favorite addition is just what is needed to sip and enjoy.

Michael Florentino wines are a match here. They have various styles of wine that are well made and go with Spanish, Italian and most foods. These are good wines to have on hand.

Warning!!! Don't forget your blankets!

Picnic at the Game

🍷 Basil Chips

🍷 Green Beans with Garlic Dip

🍷 Spaghetti Rolls

🍷 Zucchini Bread

Basil Chips

Enough for 4 guests

- 2 sprigs fresh Basil
- 4 T Olive Oil
- 1 bag Gourmet Potato Chips

---

1. In a large bowl, place basil then oil and let rest at least 8 hours.

2. Add chips and toss. Quickly remove from bowl and place onto paper towel.

3. Place chips on a baking sheet in a single layer and bake 10 to 15 minutes until chips are dry, but not brown.

4. Place in paper bag. So pack up your picnic and enjoy!

Green Beans with Garlic Dip

Enough for 4 guests

- 3 T Plain Greek Yogurt
- 3 T Sour Cream
- 2 T Mayonnaise
- 2 t fresh Garlic, chopped
- ½ t Dill, dry
- ¼ t Salt
- ¼ t Pepper
- ½ lb Green Beans, fresh

---

1. In a bowl, mix all ingredients except beans.

2. In four 12 oz jars, place dip in bottom. Stand the beans into the dip and place lid on each jar.

Handy to have at the game.

Spaghetti Rolls

Enough for 6 guests

- 4 French Rolls
- 1 lb Hamburger, browned and chunked
- 2 c Spaghetti Sauce
- 1 c Mozzarella Cheese, shredded

Preheat oven to 350 degrees

---

1. First, slice off the small end of each roll to expose the soft bread. With your fingers, pick out the center of the rolls and keep the pieces in a bowl.

2. In a large bowl, mix hamburger, sauce and cheese. Then mix in bread pieces.

3. With a spoon, stuff mixture back into the rolls. Place sliced end of roll back over hole.

4. Wrap rolls in foil and bake for 15 to 20 minutes, until warmed through.

5. Transport in lunch box cooler to keep warm.

Zucchini Bread

Enough for 2 loaves

- 3 c Flour
- 1 t Baking Powder
- 1 t Baking Soda
- 1 t Cinnamon
- 2 c Sugar
- 4 Eggs
- 1 c Oil
- 2 c Zucchini, grated
- ½ t Vanilla
- 1 c Walnuts, chopped

Preheat oven to 350 degrees

---

1. In a medium bowl, mix flour, baking powder, baking soda, and cinnamon. Set aside.

2. In another bowl, mix eggs, sugar and oil. Add zucchini, vanilla, and walnuts. Mix well.

3. Pour the wet ingredients into the flour mixture and fold them together until all parts are moist. Be careful not to over mix.

4. Butter and sugar two loaf pans. Pour batter into loaf pans.

5. Bake for 40 to 50 minutes until toothpick goes in and comes out clean.

Salad Shower

This is a shower that I threw for my daughter when she got married.

When she was young and before my son was born, we would have salad and popcorn for dinner when their dad was away for the evening. It was a big deal with us. She really thought she was getting away with something. I didn't really have to cook much but could sneak in the protein and veggies.

Even when there were more kids in the house we would have it, but it all started with my daughter, so it seemed a perfect theme for her shower. I placed the popcorn on the tables as a snack. It was just right to nibble on as she opened gifts. I completed the party with her favorite cupcakes. Angela, you will always be my pumpkin!

Even if you don't serve this menu, maybe it will inspire you to create personal, thought-out menus that mean something to the people that mean something to you!

Finn Hill Wines are my pick for this menu. They are beautiful. The flavors are light, bright and complex. Perfect for this menu. The labels are painted by a local artist, the flowers are a beautiful touch.

Salad Shower

Broccoli Salad

Pea Salad

Carrot Salad

Tortellini Salad

Caprese Salad

Popcorn

Coconut Cupcakes

Broccoli Salad

Enough for 12 guests

- 5 c Fresh Broccoli, cut into tiny pieces
- 1 c Cheddar Cheese, grated
- ⅓ c Bacon Bits, cooked
- ¼ c Raisins
- ¼ c Craisins®
- ¼ c Sunflower Seeds
- 2 c Mayonnaise
- ⅔ c Sugar

---

1. In a large bowl, add broccoli, cheese, bacon, raisins, Craisins® and sunflower seeds.

2. In a small bowl, mix mayonnaise and sugar together.

3. Pour the mayonnaise mixture over large bowl of ingredients and mix.

4. Place in a pretty bowl and serve.

Pea Salad

Enough for 12 guests

- 4 c Frozen Peas
- ¼ c Red Pepper, fine chopped
- ⅓ c Mayonnaise
- ⅓ c Sour Cream
- ½ lb Salad Shrimp
- Salt and pepper

---

1. In a large bowl add frozen peas, peppers, mayonnaise and sour cream and mix. Cover and refrigerate a minimum of 8 hours.

2. 15 minutes before you serve, mix well and drain any extra liquid. Add shrimp and mix. Add salt and pepper to taste.

Serve in a pretty glass bowl.

Carrot Salad

Enough for 12 guests

- 4 c Carrots, shredded
- 1 c Mayonnaise
- 1 c Pineapple, canned, well drained, chopped
- ¼ c Raisins, mixed colors
- Salt and Pepper

---

1. In a large bowl, mix all ingredients. Salt and pepper to taste.

This salad is best if it is prepared the night before and then drain well right before serving.

Tortellini Salad

Enough for 12 guests

- 5 c Tortellini Pasta, cooked, cooled
- ¼ c Kalamata Olives, sliced
- 2 c Cherry Tomatoes, halved
- ¼ c Red Onion, chopped
- ¼ c Green Pepper, chopped
- ½ c Olive Oil
- 3 T Red Wine Vinegar
- 1 T Dijon Mustard
- 2 t Garlic, minced
- 2 t Parsley, chopped
- Salt and Pepper
- ¼ c Parmesan Cheese, shredded

---

1. In a large bowl, add pasta, olives, tomatoes, onion, and green pepper.

2. In a small bowl add Oil, vinegar, mustard, garlic, and parsley, whisk well. Add salt and pepper to taste. Pour over vegetables in large bowl and toss.

3. Transfer salad to pretty bowl and top with cheese.

Caprese Salad

Enough for 12 guests

- 7 Tomatoes, sliced whole and thin
- 2 lb Mozzarella Cheese, fresh, sliced
- 35 Basil Leaves, cut into small strips
- ½ c Olive Oil
- ¼ c Balsamic Vinegar
- Salt and Pepper

---

1. On a large platter, lay a slice of tomato, then a slice of cheese, and alternating neatly over the platter, covering it.

2. Sprinkle the basil, oil, and vinegar randomly over the tomatoes and cheese.

3. Salt and pepper to taste.

Popcorn

Enough for 12 guests

- 3 c Popcorn, uncooked
- 2 Brown Paper Lunch Sacks
- ½ c Butter, melted
- Salt

---

1. Place 1 ½ c popcorn in 1 bag. Fold top over itself three times. Place in microwave, push popcorn setting, and cook. Pour popped corn into big fancy bowl.

2. Repeat with second bag.

3. Take remaining corn that didn't pop and repeat.

4. Pour butter over popped corn, salt to taste.

Coconut Cupcakes

Enough for 12 guests

Cupcakes:

- 1 White Cake Mix
- ⅓ c Oil
- 3 Eggs
- 1 c Water
- 1 t Vanilla
- 3 T Instant Vanilla Pudding, powder out of package
- 1 c Coconut Flakes

Frosting:

- 1 lb Butter
- 2 lb Powdered Sugar
- 1 T Vanilla Extract
- 1 T Almond Extract
- 1 t Salt
- 2 T Hot Water
- 2 c Coconut Flakes

Preheat oven to 330 degrees

Cupcakes:

1. In a large bowl, add cake mix, oil, eggs, water, vanil-

la, and pudding. and Mix with blender until smooth. With a large spoon, stir in coconut.

2. Scoop into cupcake papers, filling ¾ full.

3. Bake 16 to 18 minutes. Don't let them brown. Check with toothpick for doneness. Let cool while you make your frosting.

Frosting:

1. In a mixer, add butter, powdered sugar, salt and extracts. Pulse on slow to start. Once sugar is incorporated, blend until smooth. Add hot water to thin it slightly to make it easier to work.

2. Once cupcakes are completely cooled, frost, and top with a good amount of coconut.

Call me over so I can have one! Enjoy!

Luncheon with the Ladies

Nice on the patio, but delicious anywhere, this menu takes your palette on a rollercoaster of flavor—from sweet to green to crisp and back again, it just bursts of flavor.

Lay out loads of flowers and your best dishes. Brew your favorite tea, open your special wine, and throw some seasonal fruit in the water pitchers. Call the ladies over and enjoy the afternoon. It's a great way to bond or to thank supportive friends.

Don't you deserve it?

My wine suggestion for this menu is a wine spritzer. If you have never had one you should.

Luncheon with the Ladies

🍷 Goat Cheese and Pear Jelly

🍷 Minted Cucumber Soup

🍷 Orange Pecan Salad

🍷 French Chicken Salad

🍷 Lemon Bars

Goat Cheese and Pear Jelly

Enough for 6 guests

- 6 Pears, fresh, peeled, cored, diced
- ¼ c Water
- 2 T Lemon Juice
- 1 c Sugar
- ¼ c Pecans, chopped
- ¼ lb Goat Cheese
- 1 box Crackers

---

1. In a sauce pan, cook pears, water, lemon juice, and sugar over medium heat, stirring occasionally, until pears are easy to mash. The color should be a beautiful amber.

2. Remove from stove and mix in pecans. Pour into a jar. Refrigerate 6 hours or more.

3. Clump cheese in center of a platter. Spoon chilled jelly over cheese and serve with crackers.

Minted Cucumber Soup

Enough for 6 guests

- 4 Cucumbers, peeled, seeded
- 1 large clove Garlic
- 1 c Plain Greek Yogurt
- 2 T Lemon Juice
- ¼ c Water
- 4 Scallions, cut into 1-inch pieces
- ¾ c Fresh Mint Leaves, loosely packed
- Salt and ground black Pepper

---

1. In a food processer or a blender, add all ingredients except a few mint leaves to reserve for garnish. Blend until smooth.

2. Chill in refrigerator 2 or more hours.

3. Serve chilled, in a bowl with a leaf of mint on top.

Orange Pecan Salad

Enough for 6 guests

- ½ c Pecans, halved
- ¼ c Sugar
- ½ t Cinnamon
- Pinch Nutmeg, ground
- Pinch Cloves, ground
- Pinch Cream of Tartar
- 2 T Water
- ¾ c Mayonnaise
- ⅓ c Sugar
- 2 T Apple Cider Vinegar
- 1 T Poppy Seeds
- 4 c Mixed Greens
- ½ c Purple Cabbage, chopped
- ½ c Green Cabbage, chopped
- ¼ c Carrots, shredded
- ⅓ c Green Onions, sliced
- 1 can Mandarin Orange segments
- ¼ lb Blue Cheese, crumbled

---

1. In a sauce pan, mix sugar, cinnamon, nutmeg, cloves, cream of tartar and water. Bring to boil over medium-high heat. Boil 1 minute.

2. Mix pecans into hot mixture and lay out on wax paper to cool and dry.

3. In a small bowl, combine mayonnaise, sugar, vinegar, and poppy seeds. Mix well and set dressing aside.

4. In a large serving bowl, toss greens, cabbage, and carrots with dressing.

5. Layer green onions, oranges, cheese and cooled pecans on top.

French Chicken Salad

- 2 breast of Chicken, cooked, skinned, deboned, chopped
- 1 ½ c Grapes, seedless, sliced
- 4 stalks Celery, topped, minced
- 1 c Mayonnaise
- 2 T Herb de Provence
- 1 t Garlic, powder
- 1 T Lemon Juice
- Salt & Pepper

1. Place all in ingredients in bowl. Mix well. Add salt and pepper to taste.

Note: Can be made in advance.

Lemon Bars

Enough for 12 guests

- 2 c Flour
- 1 c Powder Sugar
- Pinch of Salt
- 1 c Butter
- 4 Eggs
- 2 c Sugar
- 6 T Flour
- 6 T Lemon Juice
- ¼ c Powder Sugar

---

1. In a medium bowl, whisk flour, sugar and salt. Cut butter in small pieces and blend with a pastry cutter. If you do not have a pastry cutter, use gloved hands to incorporate butter into flour mixture. Continue mixing until it forms a flaky crust.

2. Press into a 9" x 13", lightly greased, baking dish. Bake for 20 minutes.

3. While crust is baking, mix eggs, sugar, flour and lemon in a bowl.

4. Pour into hot crust and bake another 25 minutes.

5. When slightly cooled, dust with powdered sugar.

6. Refrigerate until ready to serve.

Turkey for Thirty

Being the youngest of three by 18 years, my brothers had their own homes and families as I was growing up. Some of my favorite times were when we all gathered together. Food was always the center of attention and there were usually around thirty people.

I learned at a young age how to work in the kitchen on Thanksgiving. In my young adult life, I attended Thanksgivings with in-laws. They were done fancy and nice, but nothing was ever as good as this menu and everyone piled on top of each other eating it. In our family, this is the menu we have always had, with everyone pitching in to bring it.

Oh, and the pie! I have included my apple pie recipe, but our normal holiday celebration has four or five different flavors. It used to be that after dinner all the ladies would clean up and then ask the men which kind of pie they would like. If they said "yeah," that meant a piece of each kind. Times have changed, new family members have come and some have passed, but the menu and the loud laughter remains the same.

For the holidays, my husband and I love hot spiced wine and spiced ciders.

A quick summary: Have each person bring something, everyone should help clean up, and make sure to add loads of love and laughter—no matter what size of space!

Turkey for Thirty

🍷 Hobby Relish Tray

🍷 Bacon Green Bean Casserole

🍷 Aunt Kathy's 24-Hour Salad

🍷 Mashed Potatoes

🍷 Home-style Gravy

🍷 Buttery Stuffing

🍷 Mom's Juicy Turkey

🍷 Apple Pie

And any other pie you can get someone to bring!

Just keep the pumpkin pie safe from Seth!

ChefAnneMarie.com

Hobby Relish Tray

Enough for 30 guests

- 8 cans Black Olives, large
- 1 jar Green Olives, pimento stuffed
- 1 jar Pickled Vegetables, drained
- 1 jar Dill Pickles, whole and drained
- 1 jar Spicy Garlic Dill Pickles, sliced and drained
- 1 jar Sweet Cucumber Chips, drained
- 1 jar Sweet Pickles, whole midget and drained
- 1 jar of Marinated Artichokes, drained and quartered
- 1 jar Pickled Asparagus, drained
- 1 can Pickled Beets, drained and sliced
- 1 lb Cherry Tomatoes

---

1. Lay two platters side by side in front of you.

2. Splitting evenly, place a pile of black olives on each platter.

Hobby children love their black olives even the young at heart. So in my family that means everyone.

3. Splitting evenly, place a pile of green olives on each platter on opposite sides of the black olives.

Hand a handful to Michael as he passes and to Kay who is probably laying out more food.

4. Splitting evenly, place a pile of pickled vegetables in

the center of each platter.

These are most loved by my brother, Steve, and his daughter, Heather.

5. Splitting evenly, place a pile of dill pickles on each platter next to the black olives.

Be careful because Skyler and Kramer may be behind you trying to sneak some.

6. Splitting evenly, place a pile of spicy garlic dill pickles on each platter next to the dill pickles.

We enjoy Angie's home-canned spicy garlic dill pickles. If you aren't blessed with an Angie in your family, you may also use Nally's.

7. Splitting evenly, place a pile of sweet cucumber chips on each platter on the other side of the olives away from the dill pickles.

Stella, Mallory, Christy and Scarlett will be begging for these.

8. Splitting evenly, place a pile of sweet pickles on each platter next to the cucumber chips.

Watch for Zac! He may smell them and come running.

9. Splitting evenly, place a pile of artichokes on each platter next to the sweet pickles.

Chad is right around the corner waiting for his special handful.

10. Splitting evenly, place a pile of pickled asparagus on each platter, next to the spicy garlic dill pickles.

Warning: Angela will eat them right out of the jar.

11. Splitting evenly, place a pile of beets on each platter next to the asparagus.

These are my mom and my favorites!

12. Splitting evenly, randomly place cherry tomatoes on each platter, spreading color over the platter.

Hopefully, Sara is close by to grab some of her favorite.

13. Cover one platter with foil and set out of the way. Place second platter on table first as before you start to lay out the feast.

When the last feast item is placed on the table and everyone has come in to do their plates, uncover and lay second platter on the table. This will insure that the football watchers will, at least, get some.

These are the things that seem to work for the Hobby's! Although the names and faces in this method will be different for you, hopefully the amount of love and memories will be the same.

Warning: You might think different next time you cook around your family.

Bacon Green Bean Casserole

Enough for 30 guests

- 1 package of Bacon, diced
- ½ c Onion, diced
- 1 c Flour
- 2 cans of Evaporated Milk
- 5 lb Green Beans, cleaned and blanched
- ¼ c Oil
- 1 c Onions, cut in thin strips
- 1 c Flour

---

1. In a good-sized, nonstick fry pan, brown bacon bits over medium heat. One minute or so before bacon becomes crispy, add diced onions

2. When the onions are clear, add flour, enough to soak up the bacon fat. Stir constant for another minute or two. You are trying to cook the flour just a little. This makes a roux (thickener). Add milk, stirring constantly. You may add a little water if it's too thick. Now you have your white sauce. Taste it to see if you want to add salt and pepper. Your call.

3. In a baking dish, place blanched beans and pour sauce over and mix.

4. Clean the fry pan and add oil over medium heat.

5. While the oil heats, lightly flour onion strips. Add to

hot oil. Cook the onions until crispy, then place on a paper towel to drain.

6. Place drained onion crisps over top of beans.

7. Bake uncovered for about 20 to 25 minutes.

Or you can make the Old fashion Green Bean Casserole I grew up on!

- 3 cans Cream of Mushroom Soup, Campbell's only
- 4 cans Green Beans, drained, not low salt or French cut
- 1 can French Fried Onions, French's

1. Preheat oven to 350

2. In a baking dish, mix soup and beans. Pour onions over top.

3. Bake for 20 to 30 minutes, in a 350 oven until sides bubble.

I do like both and switch back and forth between which one to make. A tradition is a tradition at the Hobby's.

Aunt Kathy's 24-Hour Salad

Enough for 30 guests

- 2 heads Iceberg Lettuce, chopped
- 8 stalks of Celery, sliced
- 2 cans Water Chestnuts, sliced
- 2 c Green Peas, frozen
- 5 Green Onions, sliced
- 3 c Mayonnaise
- 2 c Sugar
- 1 c Cheddar Cheese, shredded
- ½ c Bacon, cooked, chopped

---

1. In a large glass bowl layer Lettuce, celery, chestnuts, peas, and green onions

2. In a small bowl Mix Mayonnaise and sugar then spread it over peas

3. Refrigerate for a minimum of 8 hours, 24 hrs is preferred things will melt and this is good.

4. Just before you serve it toss the salad and top with cheese and bacon.

Mashed Potatoes

Enough for 30 guests

- 10 lb Potatoes, peeled, large cubes
- 1 lb Butter, large cubes
- 2 c Cream or Milk, I use cream on a special occasion
- Salt and Pepper

---

1. In a large pot add potatoes and cover with cold water
2. Bring to a boil over high heat
3. In a small pan warm milk or cream. Do not boil
4. Boil potatoes until fork can sink into them easily
5. Turn burner off. Drain water from potatoes and set back on hot burner.
6. Once extra moisture has steamed off add ¾ of the butter and give it couple of minutes to start melting
7. With a potato masher or large spoon mash the potato and butter together
8. Add ½ of the warm cream and mix with a mixer
9. If the potatoes seem hard to mix then add more cream in small amounts
10. Whip until smooth and creamy
11. Salt and pepper to taste (Matthew's favorite!)

Home-Style Gravy

Enough for 30 guests

- 6 to 7 c Stock *
- 1 cup Cold Water
- ⅔ c Flour
- Salt and Pepper

---

1. In a pan over high heat, bring stock to a boil. It is up to you if you strain the liquid first. My family we likes all the bits and pieces from the turkey to be in our gravy, hence the Home-Style.

2. In a cup (I use a coffee cup at home), mix water and flour with a fork. Add the mixture to the stock and stir stock right away. For lump prevention, be sure to stir the flour as you pour it into the stock.

3. Bring the gravy back to a rolling boil, stirring constantly. Cook for at least 3 minutes. If you like thicker gravy, add more flour but make sure to use the water method.

4. Salt and pepper to taste with my top taster Andrew!

---

* For Thanksgiving, I use the liquids from the cooked turkey. If I need more, I add chicken stock. I also like the liquids from a roast or good chicken stock when doing a gravy for a roast. This is a classic all-purpose gravy recipe.

Buttery Stuffing

Enough for 30 guests

- 6 loaves Herbed Focaccia Bread, small cubes
- 7 c Chicken Stock
- ½ lb Butter
- 2 large Onions, diced
- 7 stalks Celery, chopped
- 2 T Rosemary, chopped
- 2 T Thyme
- 4 T Sage, ground
- ½ lb Butter, cubed

Preheat oven to 350 degrees

---

1. Place bread cubes on a cookie sheet and toast, Make sure the cubes are dry. This is key to your success. Set aside.

2. In a pot, bring stock to a boil and keep warm.

3. In a large-bottomed pan, add butter and onion. Cook 3 minutes. Add celery and cook another 3 minutes. Add rosemary, thyme and sage and cook 1 more minute.

4. In a large baking pan, add bread, butter, and vegetable mixture. Mix together. Slowly, add one ladle of stock

at a time, mixing bread as you go. Amounts will vary. You want to moisten the bread, but not drown it.

5. Place butter cubes around the top and bake until the top is toasted, about 20 to 25 minutes.

Mom's Juicy Turkey

Enough for 30 guests

- 18 to 20 lb Turkey, thawed, rinsed
- ½ Butter, cubed
- 2 T Garlic, granules
- 2 whole Onions, peeled
- 2 T Rosemary, chopped
- 2 T Thyme,
- 4 T Sage, ground
- Salt and Pepper
- 4 c Chicken Stock

Preheat oven to 425 degrees

---

1. In a large Roasting pan place turkey. Make sure all the extra pieces are out of both sides of the cavity. Stuff onions in the body cavity.

2. With the breast up, use your hand and lay butter cubes under skin, pressing down to smash as you go

3. Sprinkle entire outside of bird with herbs, garlic, salt and pepper

4. Pour stock in bottom of pan

5. Bake turkey uncovered for 20 minutes then cover

tight with foil, drop oven to 350 degrees and continue cooking another 3 to 3 ½ hours. If you desire it browner Turkey remove foil your last 15 to 20 minutes of baking. You need to check you turkey putting the thermometer in the thickest meat, between the thigh and the breast, not the top of the breast. You want it to be 155 degrees because it will come up another 5 to 7 degrees as you rest it on the counter, covered for 10 minutes.

Don't forget to save those drippings for the gravy.

Apple Pie

Enough for 30 guests

Crust:

- 4 c Flour
- 1 t Salt
- 4 t Sugar
- 1 ⅓ c Butter, cubed and cold
- 8 T cold Water
- 8 T Egg, scrambled with fork
- 8 t Vinegar
- ½ c Flour

Filling:

- 12 large Apples, peeled, cored, and sliced
- ¼ c Cinnamon
- ¼ c Sugar
- ¼ c Flour
- ½ c Butter, cubed and cold
- Egg wash

Preheat oven to 350 degrees

1. In a large bowl, mix flour, salt, and sugar.

2. With a pastry blender, two knives, or gloved hands,

cut the butter into the flour to create pea-sized chunks.

3. With a fork, mix in water, egg, and vinegar until dough starts to form then press together with your hands.

4. Let dough rest 5 minutes

5. On a floured surface, cut dough into 4 balls. Roll out each ball evenly to a 12-inch circle. Place 2 of them into pie pans.

6. In a large bowl, mix apples, cinnamon, and sugar. Add flour to thicken. The amount of flour will depend upon the juiciness of the apples.

7. Fill pie shells heaping, because with the apples will bake down—so really heap it.

8. Lay cubes of butter randomly around apples.

9. Place the pie dough on top and cut shapes to vent apples. Be creative. Crimp edges and brush egg wash on top.

10. Bake for 60 to 80 minutes. Until apples are soft. Test with a fork.

About the Author

Anne Marie finished culinary school in1996 and has been working in all dimensions of the culinary industry since. Having been a member of the Washington State Chefs Association has allowed her to be blessed with the opportunity to work alongside the best of the best—including 2 James Beard award-winning chefs.

Loving most foods and having been a caterer as well as a mother most of her career, Anne Marie finds it hard to define her food style. "It's all about what the customer wants," she has been heard to say many times. She has catered from 2 to 500 guests and worked from fast food to fine dining. Anne Marie's passion lies in creating a completely unique and customizable experience to fit each customer's food desires.

She also finds passion in teaching culinary skills. Anne Marie believes that to know cooking is to love cooking. Food is the common thing in everyone's life. It's something we need every day! Why not make it wonderful?

You can find Chef Anne Marie and her cooking classes on ChefAnneMarie.com

Chef Anne Marie's Inspirations

Ina Garten (Barefoot Contessa) – Anne Marie's education in fine dining allows her to appreciate the knowledge and twists on the classics which Ina makes. She also admires the use of seasonal fresh ingredients that Ina uses in the parties she throws. Another way in which Anne Marie and Ina really connect is that they can both cook as well as they bake. Truly classic women!

Chef Russell Lowell – Working with Russell taught Anne Marie to be about standards and to stick to her guns to demand excellence. He also showed her how to value her employees and clients as if they are family. Anne Marie felt it was a great treasure to be a part of his grand affairs, restaurants, and charity events.

Chef Tom Douglas – While working with Tom on a charity event in 1995, he graciously gave Anne Marie a tour of the Dahlia Lounge at its original location about one block from where it is now. It was small, but spectacular! He actually had plates with his special design for his menu items. At that time, Tom was beginning to open Etta's, named after his daughter. Currently, he owns 12 restaurants while still being the same down-to-earth, creative person. His entrepreneurial enterprises and cooking expertise have been great influences on both Anne Marie

and the entire Seattle dining scene.

Chef Kathy Casey – Being Kathy's chief bottle washer and girl Friday while in college was a super ride on a food design train for Anne Marie. If 50 tests were needed for the same item to get the recipe right, Kathy and Anne Marie performed 50 tests! If they were working on pastries, Kathy would hire a pastry expert to assist in creating a perfect confection. Kathy taught Anne Marie to look at every angle and to be creative. She also introduced Anne Marie to some amazing people who enhanced her cooking experience so she could become the chef she is today.

Chef Chuck Gibbs – Chef Chuck is seafood! Working with Chuck was like spending time with a friend. He shared cooking techniques and purchasing knowledge while making it enjoyable. Chuck made it easy for Anne Marie to feel confident in her seafood preparation skills.

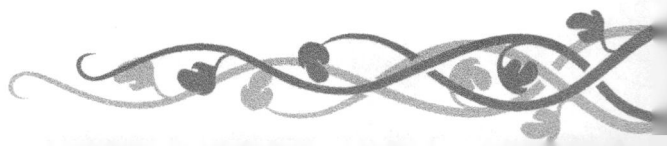

Index